Notting Hill Editions is an independent British publisher. The company was founded by Tom Kremer (1930–2017), champion of innovation and the man responsible for popularising the Rubik's Cube.

After a successful business career in toy invention Tom decided, at the age of eighty, to fulfil his passion for literature. In a fast-moving digital world Tom's aim was to revive the art of the essay, and to create exceptionally beautiful books that would be cherished.

Hailed as 'the shape of things to come', the family-run press brings to print the most surprising thinkers of past and present. In an era of information-overload, these collectible pocket-size books distil ideas that linger in the mind.

Tom McCarthy is a novelist whose work has been translated into more than twenty languages and adapted for cinema, theatre and radio. In 2013 he was awarded one of the inaugural Windham Campbell Prizes for fiction. His first novel, *Remainder*, won the 2007 *Believer* Book Award; his third, *C*, was a 2010 Booker Prize finalist, as was his fourth, *Satin Island*, in 2015. He is also author of the study *Tintin and the Secret of Literature*, and of the essay collection *Typewriters, Bombs, Jellyfish*. His latest novel, *The Making of Incarnation*, was published in 2021.

McCarthy has held Visiting Professorships at the Royal College of Art in London, Columbia University in New York and Städelschule in Frankfurt. Since 2022 he has held the position of Miller Scholar at the Santa Fe Institute, New Mexico. In 2019 he guest-curated the exhibition 'Empty House of the Stare' at London's Whitechapel Gallery, and in 2022 a major exhibition, 'Holding Pattern', in Kunstnernes Hus, Oslo, responding to the art institute's invitation to explore the themes and motifs of his work. Born in Scotland, he is now a Swedish citizen, and lives in Berlin.

THE THRESHOLD AND THE LEDGER

—

Tom McCarthy

Notting Hill Editions

Published in 2025
by Notting Hill Editions Ltd
Mirefoot, Burnside, Kendal LA8 9AB

Series and cover design by Tom Etherington

Typeset by CB Editions, London
Printed and bound in the UK by Clays Ltd, Elcograf S.p.A.

The publisher is grateful for permission to quote from the following:
Ingeborg Bachmann, 'Salz und Brot', from *Die gestundete Zeit*. Copyright
©1978, 2000 by Piper Verlag GmbH, München. Reprinted with the
permission of Bonnier Media Deutschland GmbH. Translation copyright
© 2006 by Peter Filkins from *Darkness Spoken: Ingeborg Bachmann, The
Collected Poem*s. Reprinted with the permission of The Permissions
Company, LLC on behalf of Zephyr Press, zephyrpress.org.

A CIP record for this book is available from the British Library

ISBN 978-1-912559-67-1

nottinghilleditions.com

To the staff and fellows – past, present and future
– of the DAAD Artists-in-Berlin Program,
of which both Ingeborg Bachmann and I have
been beneficiaries.

Contents

Ingeborg Bachmann was born in the provincial Austrian town of Klagenfurt in 1926 and died in Rome in 1973. In the short span of her lifetime, she managed to bag the lion's share of the German-ophone literary prizes and get nominated for the Nobel; play a vocal role, through her lectures, radio work and membership of the influential Gruppe 47, in the cultural and political reshaping of German society after the catastrophe of World War Two; become romantically entangled with such luminaries as Paul Celan, Max Frisch and – improbably but truly – Henry Kissinger (whom she met when he organised a symposium for European intellectuals in 1955, although she seems to have cooled on him during his carpet bombing-advocacy phase); and, not least, publish two volumes of poetry that, by any reckoning, must take their place among the most important of the post-war period in any language, never mind German. I want to begin this book, written on the eve of her centenary, by homing in on a poem that appears towards the end of *Borrowed Time*, the first of these two collections, published in 1953.

In the second stanza of 'Salt and Bread', Bachmann writes (and here, as throughout, I turn to Peter Filkins's excellent Zephyr Press translation):

Into the hand of my oldest friend
I place the key to my post; the rain man will now manage
my darkened house and lengthen
the lines of the ledger which I drew up
since I stayed less often.

The words, like so many of Bachmann's, are obtuse, elliptical, reluctant to offer themselves up for instant comprehension. Nonetheless, they give us things to work with: images, contexts, allusions. The poem's title points us to the German custom, known as *Brot und Salz*, whereby neighbours, friends and relatives bring bread and salt to welcome people into a new house. Bachmann, though, has inverted the ritual's order: *Salz und Brot*. In her telling, salt comes first, then bread. The reversal extends to the whole scenario: the sequence being painted here is one of departure, not arrival; moving *out* rather than in; shutting up shop; closing a house down, passing its keys and general management over to someone else rather than assuming it oneself. But then, a few stanzas later, we get a second reversal:

> So I gather the salt
> when the sea overcomes us,
> and turn back
> and lay it on the threshold
> and step into the house.

The poem's narrator, the 'I'-figure, seems to have had a change of mind, or at least destination, back to the home that she relinquished earlier. Returning to it, she takes on the role of, initially, welcoming neighbour, laying salt on its threshold, then, again, inhabitant, stepping across this threshold, back inside. Her re-entry, though, rather than restituting to her full domestic mastery, inaugurates a kind of joint-accommodation set-up. The poem's final couplet reads:

> We share bread with the rain;
> bread, a debt, and a house.

You'll notice that the 'I' has become 'we': this new arrangement is a general condition. What does it mean for us to share our house with rain? Symbolically, it implies a structural rupture: breach of a dividing membrane, an opening of inside to outside (private to public, individual to collective, human to inhuman or elemental). More basically, at the most literal level, it just means our roof is broken.

This book will be a slow unpacking of these twelve lines. It will involve, like Bachmann's poem, a set of digressions, of departures and returns. To put it more viscerally (or perhaps eviscerally): as with the house that Bachmann invites us to imagine, the poem's inside will be laid open to the many scenes and histories – collective, elemental, frequently inhuman – that amass, burst and drizzle, drive or hurtle down towards it from beyond its borders.

L et's begin, then, by unpacking the poem's central, overriding frame and setting – namely, the motif of the house. Near the outset of *The Poetics of Space*, his wonderful examination (published in 1958) of the many ways in which human experience is shaped – and haunted – by its topological and architectural substrata, the philosopher Gaston Bachelard informs us:

Now my aim is clear: I must show that the house is one of the greatest powers of integration for the thoughts, memories and dreams of mankind . . . Past, present and future give the house different dynamisms, which often interfere, at times opposing, at others, stimulating one another. In the life of a man, the house thrusts aside contingencies, its councils of continuity are unceasing. Without it, man would be a dispersed being.

That's what the house is *meant* to do, at least. But I would supplement Bachelard's observation with a contingent, or contending, one made by another figure from whom we'll be hearing intermittently: the film-maker David Lynch, who, in an interview with the critic Chris Rodley (one of a series published in 1997 under the title *Lynch on Lynch*), deploying the equally wonderful surrealism-meets-gee-whizz-folksy idiom he made his own, sums up the starting premise of so much of his work with the simple line: 'The house is a place where things can go wrong.'

Both Bachelard's and Lynch's propositions are, of course, true. Or, to phrase this assertion with logical preciseness: neither proposition is entirely true unless it comes in cohort with the other, even if they clash or pull in opposite directions. This ambivalent capacity of the house, its double-tendency towards shelter and integration (on the one hand) and (on the other) strife and destructiveness, has fuelled drama, poetry and the novel for centuries. It drives, for example, the entire corpus of Greek tragedy, which is never *really* about its various heroes but rather about the house of which these heroes are mere iterations, symptoms you could almost say: the House of Atreus (in Aeschylus's Oresteian cycle, to which we'll be turning shortly); the House of Thebes (in Sophocles's

Theban one) and so forth. Indeed, the Greek word for 'house', *oikos*, has a dual meaning: family over several generations *and* physical house, its bricks and columns. The one encloses or contains the other. (*Oikos* is also the root of the word *economics*, conceived at its outset as the reach and domain of a house or family, extended beyond the property's physical boundary through trade and its attendant, expanded networks of credit and debt.)

And now, as promised, to the *Oresteia*. No matter how many times I think or write about this trilogy (*Agamemnon*, *The Libation Bearers* and *The Eumenides*, all originally performed in 458 BC), I can't help coming back to it over and over, each revisit yielding new returns – its bounty is endless. When the first of its three parts opens, the patriarch Atreus has been dead for many years; but his house is both the subject and the setting of most of the action that will follow. A lookout, standing on its roof, picks up a beacon-signal announcing Troy's downfall and the imminent seaborne return of the house's (and the city-state of Argos's) current, if absent, master, Atreus's son Agamemnon, who's been off for the last ten years fighting. While the lookout shouts the tidings from the rooftop, other chorus members, placed lower in both altitude and order of enunciation, gather before the house's entrance and, through murmur and insinuation, trade rumours about the royal family's history. If the roof is the platform from which the 'official' news gets broadcast, the nether floors provide the stage set for the dissemination of more coded signals, incomplete accounts of hushed-up crimes. The nature of these crimes comes into focus as the play progresses, and it reads like a charge-sheet of unspeakability: incest, infanticide, fratricide, cannibalism – the lot. Atreus's twin brother Thyestes, it turns out, besides regularly copulating with Atreus's wife Aerope, also fathered children with his own daughter Pelopia. Atreus, on finding this out, butchered these children, fed them to an unwitting Thyestes, then, revealing all, murdered him too. All these things went wrong in this house. Their secret histories are at once stored in its walls *and* leaking from them, like radioactivity from a reactor sealed in a thick concrete sarcophagus in the wake of a catastrophic meltdown but still (since all seals are imperfect) slowly and inexorably oozing out, at levels high enough to register on a good Geiger counter.

Cassandra, the Trojan princess brought back home by Agamemnon as a trophy, acts as just this type of high-end, sensitive device. Equipped with special powers of intuition, she's immediately able to pick up and amplify the house's dark, muted emissions or (to switch from a radioactive to a straight radio analogy) transmissions. Entering soon after the play begins with Agamemnon and his entourage, welcomed by his wife Clytemnestra (who, nursing a much deeper cause for resentment towards her husband, is relatively unbothered by his acquisition of a captive mistress), Cassandra tunes in to these transmissions, and starts giving voice, in broken sentences, garbled chains of images and exclamations, to the leaked traces of both past and future. She has visions of the bathtub in which she and her lover/master will soon (as Clytemnestra has planned) be murdered; also of the house's victims who preceded her, the children of Thyestes. 'What house have you got me to?' she enquires incredulously of Agamemnon. It's illuminating to compare Philip Vellacott's translation of her lines, from 1956, to that by Anne Carson from just over a half-century later, in 2009. In Vellacott's rendering, Cassandra blasts the building as:

a house that hates
The gods; whose very stones

Bear guilty witness to a bloody act;
    That hides within these gates
    Remnants of bodies hacked,
    And murdered children's bones!

In Carson's, these lines morph to:

Godhated so
    then too
        much knowing together self–
            murder man-
                chop blood-
                    slop floor

I think both are great. But Carson, affording herself more poetic licence, captures the speech's force by channelling (perhaps counterintuitively and certainly anachronistically but for all that brilliantly) the twentieth-century avant-garde – the collaged word-paintings of Gertrude Stein, the cut-ups of William Burroughs – and, in doing so, manages to find a frequency we could describe as *liminal*. I use that word in both its psychoanalytical and architectural senses. It's the Anglicised adjectival form of the Latin *limen* – threshold, doorstep, sill – which was coopted into the professional lexicon of neurologists in the mid-nineteenth century to denote (as the Oxford English Dictionary puts it) 'the limit below which a given stimulus ceases to be perceptible'. What Carson amplifies in Cassandra is the way she locks onto and retransmits a kind of liminal wavelength, one that we might call – using another loaded word – *encrypted*. To run through the etymology again: *kryptos* in Greek means hidden, concealed, sealed, encased or buried in a manner that allows the buried object to be retrieved – or, indeed, revivified – later, like a human soul laid with its body in a tomb awaiting reanimation in the Christian or Egyptian afterlives, or information in a code. Atreus's house is cryptic in this double sense: a crypt stuffed full of bodies and a palimpsest on which secrets have been written in encrypted form. And, as such, it permits a two-way traffic, in and out, allowing secrets to be first buried and then disinterred, decrypted, drawn back over the threshold of intelligibility, made to speak. The chorus act as its first operators – to return to our radio conceit, they crank the dial, trawl through the spectrum until they hit on its illicit channel; then Cassandra commandeers that role, and does it much more loudly and dramatically, her phrases jarring and discordant, broken up by interference, static and white noise. Even the chorus complain that they 'have no key' to her fragmented exclamations, that she must be 'insane, or god-possessed', performing 'this wail' for no one but herself (in Carson's version, 'mad – godstruck godswept / godnonsensical / and you keep making that sound, it's not / musical'). The secrets are made to speak – but in a form that keeps their liminality intact, their condition of being on the border of the incomprehensible, the unspeakable.

I n the last passage, we've run up – stumbled almost – against a central prop in Bachmann's poem: you'll recall that 'Salt and Bread's narrator lays the sea's salt on the *threshold* of her house (now her and the rain's house) as she re-enters it. This motif, no less than that of the house, calls for a vigorous unpacking. The illustrious literary critic Mikhail Bakhtin, reflecting on Dostoevsky's handling of domestic space in his 1929 study *Problems of Dostoevsky's Poetics*, identifies the threshold as its organising feature, the central one of a set (foyer, landing, stairway) that, together,

take on the meaning of a 'point' where *crisis*, radical change, an unexpected turn of fate takes place, where decisions are made, where the forbidden line is overstepped, where one is renewed or perishes. Action in Dostoevsky's works occurs primarily at these 'points'. The interior spaces of a house or of rooms, spaces distant from the boundaries, that is from the threshold, are

almost never used by Dostoevsky . . . First of all, Rask-
olnikov lives, in essence, on a threshold: his narrow
room, a 'coffin' (a carnival symbol here) opens directly
onto the *landing of the staircase*, and he never locks his
door, even when he goes out (that is, his room is unenclosed interior space) . . . The threshold, the foyer, the
corridors, the landing, the stairway, its steps, doors
opening onto the stairway, gates to front and back yards
. . . This is the space of the novel. And in fact nothing
here ever loses touch with the threshold . . .

Bachelard, too, accords the threshold a priv-
ileged spot in his typology of space: recalling
the Greek philosopher Porphyry's claim that 'a
threshold is a sacred thing', he suggests that every
door should have a 'threshold god' incarnated
(that is, carved) in it. But above all, for Bachelard
the threshold is *poetic*: 'The poet,' he boldly
announces, 'speaks on the threshold of being.'
Walter Benjamin, in his giant, unfinished *Arcades
Project*, written between 1927 and his death on the
Franco-Spanish border in 1940, also gives much
thought to the question of the threshold. In German, threshold is *Schwelle* – Bachmann uses this
word in her poem – which, in contrast to the English emphasis on footfall (*thresh* comes from the

Anglo-Saxon *þerscan* or *thrash*, meaning 'tread' or 'trample'), captures the way the ground swells as it rises to form a sill (interestingly, Emily Dickinson makes the same intuitive association in her poem 'Because I could not stop for Death', when she describes 'a House that seemed / A Swelling of the Ground'). Benjamin is careful to draw a distinction between a threshold and a boundary: where the latter separates two territories, the former, being made up of 'transformation, passage, wave action', is more of 'a zone of transition'. For all three thinkers, though, the threshold serves a vital function in the make-up of social, symbolic and psychic space; a passage of intensity and transformation, even transfiguration, opening to the metaphysical; a space that, when traversed or hovered over, makes poetry possible; a critical place, a place of crisis; one where being meets non-being, that maintains an intimate relationship with death.

So it is with the threshold of the House of Atreus. Beckoning Agamemnon and Cassandra towards it, Clytemnestra unfurls a crimson cloth and lays this, ritually, across the doorstep, likening it as she does so to the blood-stained sea:

There is the sea and who shall drain it dry?
It breeds the purple stain, the dark red dye
    we use to colour our garments,
costly as silver.
This house has an abundance.

(Carson again.) Clytemnestra seems to have read her Benjamin: her threshold is all wave action. By contrast, Agamemnon is more Anglo-Saxon, hesitant (as he tells her) to 'trample luxuries underfoot'. Cassandra, for her part, is a Bakhtinian: she recognises this boundary as a point of crisis, a lethal border, a limit beyond which she and Agamemnon won't survive, likening its columns, jambs and lintel to 'the gates of Hades' and prophesying that 'I am soon to hit the ground'. She's absolutely right: hardly have she and Agamemnon overcome their hesitation, stepped across the threshold and entered the bath that Clytemnestra's drawn for them when they're stabbed to death by Clytemnestra, who's working in cahoots with her new lover Aegisthus. Clytemnestra's wreaking her revenge for yet another act of infanticide, one that took place beyond the house's walls: Agamemnon, in order to tame the tempestuous winds preventing the Greek ships from setting forth to Troy ten years ago, sacrificed their daughter Iphigenia on the beach at Aulis. Aegisthus, the sole surviving child of Thyestes, has a double motive for collaborating with her: to avenge his father's murder by Agamemnon's father and to usurp Agamemnon's place as king of Argos. In a way, though, these particulars are incidental: from a structural and symbolic point of view, I'd argue, it's the threshold *itself* that – like a tripwire mine or fly-killing electric zap-beam – brings about the couple's execution as they breech its line.

In fact, I'm so convinced of this that twenty years ago I wrote a version of the play in which the door-sill plays the lead role, standing alone on stage while Agamemnon's trip (in my version he stubs his toe and trips) across it is projected in super-slow, frame-per-second motion, as in Douglas Gordon's *24 Hour Psycho*. That's all that happens. It's probably the work of mine with which I'm most content – not least as it achieved the (to me, since while I love reading drama I avoid like plague going to the theatre, especially the English theatre with its endless – and very un-Greek – adherence to dumb-ass doctrines of naturalism and 'authenticity'; besides which I'm not sure if I or anybody else would actually want to sit through this) considerable feat of being reviewed (in the *London Review of Books*) without ever being performed.

But to return to Aeschylus's version: he's not done with Atreus's threshold even after *Agamemnon*'s wrapped up. He sets the cycle's next play, *The Libation Bearers*, on it too, having Agamemnon's and Clytemnestra's son Orestes turn up disguised as a stranger and, availing himself of the hospitality so sacrosanct to ancient Greeks, murder his accommodating mother as *he* steps across it, revenge for the revenge. The final instalment, *The Eumenides*, takes place on the threshold of Athens, where Orestes, pursued by vengeful Furies (supernatural creatures howling for revenge for the revenge for the revenge), pleads for asylum. The ensuing move by the city's patron goddess Athena to empower twelve of her citizens to hear both sides of the argument (Orestes's and the Furies') and then come to a decision themselves about whether or not to grant his plea – effectively, her invention of the world's first ever trial by jury – establishes an order of juridical justice, blueprint for the modern civic democracy that survives (just about) to this day. This whole chain of events, and its legacy, happens on, and proceeds from, the threshold.

It's not only Aeschylus. This type of topology

and sequence of displacement – Argos to Troy to Argos, Argos to Athens and so forth – is typical of virtually all Greek tragedy and epic poetry. Oedipus moves from Thebes to Corinth to Thebes, returning (like Orestes, although in Oedipus's case even *he* doesn't know his true identity) as a stranger. Odysseus, too, leaves his home, also in order to come back to it as a stranger. Simplifying the map of *Agamemnon* by removing Aulis and Troy from the equation, we could say that all that Agamemnon really does is move from the inside of his house to the outside of his house and back again – an observation which prompts a loop back to David Lynch. I'm thinking of his 1997 film *Lost Highway*. This 'neo-noir' work consists of two on-the-surface separate but in fact interlinked plots. The second, in which a young man finds himself embroiled in an affair with the older girlfriend of the gangster who's quasi-adopted him, has obvious Oedipal overtones; but it's the first that interests me here. In it a couple, Fred and Renee Madison, find, on the doorstep of their bunker-like house in Los Angeles (Lynch's own, as it happens), a video cassette. Slotting it into their VHS player, they see this same house filmed from outside, looming ever larger as the camera nears its facade. A second cassette arrives shortly thereafter, showing again the house's exterior – and then, after a patch of static, its interior, complete with themselves, Fred and Renee, asleep on their bed.

Unsurprisingly, they call the cops, who come and inspect the door, the windows, skylights – all the weak spots of the building's protective cara- pace, possible points of ingress – but find no sign of a break-in. A day or so later, the couple attend a party, at which Fred gets talking to a short, pale- faced man who seems familiar – and is: back home, Fred had a fleeting vision of his face superimposed on that of Renee. This Mystery Man (that's how he's billed in the film's credits) informs Fred that they've met before; when Fred demurs, asking just where it is he thinks they've met, he tells him: 'at your house', adding 'As a matter of fact, I'm there right now'. There follows what, for me, is one of the most unsettling sequences in the history of cinema as the Mystery Man hands Fred his mobile phone and tells him: 'Call me.' Fred dials his home number; sure enough, the receiver is picked up, the Mystery Man's voice comes on and confirms – even while, here at the party, this same voice's owner is staring at Fred silently – that yes, he's in his house. To Fred's subsequent question 'How did you get in?' the voice responds: 'You invited me. It is not my custom to go where I am not wanted', before, in a comic coda, adding: 'Give me back my phone.'

Things get darker still from here: at home later, Fred, alone this time, receives a third porch-dropped video. This one, shot entirely inside the house, shows him, Fred, chopping Renee into pieces, before abruptly dropping away *qua* video sequence to reveal its scenario – a blood-spattered Fred holding up Renee's severed limbs – as the actual one Fred's currently experiencing: he's murdered Renee, and the same cops have come back to arrest him. Fred, slipping ever since the outset of the film into what Lynch and his scriptwriting partner Barry Gifford describe in interviews as a 'fugue state', has peopled his unravelling psyche with various scenes and personae: the Mystery Man was an uncanny (in German, *unheimlich* or 'unhomely') alter-ego of himself, permitting him to peel back the membranes of both domicile and consciousness, embody and observe these from beyond his own point of perception, thus turning both home and psyche, to borrow Bakhtin's oxymoronic but apt formulation, into 'unenclosed interior space'.

The *Unheimlich*, as Freud points out in a

1919 paper of the same name, is a sly misnomer: uncanny things are unsettling not because they're completely alien to us but rather because (like the Mystery Man's face) they're secretly – or cryptically – familiar. Lynch's sequence may seem uncanny in part due to its extraordinary originality; but in another sense its logic is very familiar. In fact, watching it for the first time, I got a disturbing sense of déjà vu. It took me a while – some years – to pinpoint it, but I eventually did: Lynch's scene is, in essence, a reprise of one from Kafka's short text *The Burrow*, written six months before Kafka's death in 1924. The story (if we can call it that; nothing really 'happens' as such) is narrated by some kind of subterranean creature – perhaps a vole – who talks us through the layout and construction of the labyrinthine lair, replete with tunnels, dummy chambers, trap doors leading to more tunnels, and so on, which he or she has just completed. No furry innocent, this creature is a vicious, territorial carnivore; the burrow is full of intruders' and prey's dismembered flesh; its surfaces, like those of Atreus's and Fred Madison's houses, are awash with blood. At the same time, the creature, well aware that any predator can just as easily turn into prey themselves, takes great care to camouflage the burrow's entrance; indeed, so obsessed does he or she become with this task that, to be sure that this threshold (and thus the existence of the burrow *tout court*) has been rendered undetectable, he or she spends nights in the open – vulnerable to the very owls, foxes and so forth the burrow has been built to guard him or her from – looking at it, or rather at the spot where it's no longer visible. To see him- or herself safe *inside*, he or she must be *outside*. As Kafka writes:

I seek out a good hiding place and keep watch on the entrance of my house – this time from outside – for whole days and nights. Call it foolish if you like; it gives me infinite pleasure and reassures me. At such times it is as if I were not so much looking at my house as at myself sleeping, and had the joy of being in a profound slumber and simultaneously of keeping vigilant guard over myself.

Looking at both his house and himself sleeping, being both in slumber and in vigilant guard over himself is, of course, exactly what Fred Madison, in his psychosis, his fugue state, is doing too. It's interesting to note, though, that even nerdy types who try to plot and map what's 'really' happening in Lynch's film (the internet is full of these) can't square the circle: no matter how deranged Fred may be, it's still physically impossible for him to have filmed himself asleep. The very explainer, the 'reveal', far from overhauling the formless confusion of a mystery with the ordering grid of reason, institutes a logic which is utterly *illogical* and yet offers us no option but to accept it *as* the logic driving the reality it reveals and explains. *Lost Highway*, rather than simply depicting a psychotic character, elevates the state of psychosis to the organising frame and force field of its universe.

– 4 –

O ut for in – home, body, person – and in for out: this is psychosis. But we could also look at it another way, come at the situation by way of another adjective: not *psychotic* but *ecstatic*. I'm using the term here in its literal sense: *ec-stasis*, standing outside. Carson, who beside being a classical translator is also a poet and essayist whom I wouldn't be surprised to see shortlisted for the Nobel herself sooner or later, has much to say about this word. In her fantastically hybrid 2005 book *Decreation*, she reflects on the Greek poet Sappho's *Fragment 31* (interestingly, the very same fragment invoked by the novelist Rachel Kushner in her 2019 foreword to the New Directions English reprint of Bachmann's novel *Malina*, of which more later). This fragment's narrator, watching the woman she loves caught up in conversation with a man, writes (the translation is Carson's too):

> shaking
> grips me all, greener than grass
> I am and dead – or almost
> I seem to me.

The sentiment being described here, Carson asserts, is not (as it might seem at first) jealousy, but rather ecstasy:

This is not just a moment of revealed existence: it is a spiritual event. Sappho enters into ecstasy. 'Greener than grass I am . . .', she says, predicating of her own Being an attribute observable only from outside her own body. This is the condition called *ekstasis*, literally 'standing outside of oneself', a condition regarded by the Greeks as typical of mad persons, geniuses and lovers, and ascribed to poets by Aristotle.

Sappho's fragment has a final, incomplete line:

> But all is to be dared, because even a person of
> poverty

Carson, glossing this one, breaks its thought into two parts: 'The content of the thought,' she writes, 'is absolute daring. The condition of the

thought,' she continues, 'is poverty.' That economics – *oikonomeia* – rears its head here is intriguing.
Carson doesn't address its presence straight away,
but rather slides the time-cursor forwards almost
two millennia, to the mediaeval mystic Marguerite
Porete and her affirmation of a love for God 'whose
effect is to expose her very Being to its own scru-
tiny and to dislodge it from the centre of itself' –
again, ec-stasis – and then slides it further forwards
still, to twentieth-century philosopher Simone Weil
(about whom Bachmann wrote a radio-essay too,
in 1955). It's from Weil that Carson's book takes
its title: *decreation* is Weil's neologism for 'undo-
ing the creature in us', for expelling herself 'from a
centre where she cannot stay because staying there
blocks God'. Weil calls this 'a withdrawal from my
own soul'; she also describes it (and here we stum-
ble back across the economic register) as a kind of
giving, or paying, back of borrowed being.

My friend and erstwhile collaborator Simon
Critchley has recently published a very good book
on mediaeval mystics and their modern progeny,
and I direct you towards it if you want to explore
the subject further. For my part, I want to propose
a secular example of this ec-static if impoverished
(or impoverishing) standing outside of oneself:

Shakespeare's *Twelfth Night, or What You Will*
– in particular, the figure of Viola. A well-to-do
young lady of Messaline, Viola, finding herself
shipwrecked on the coast of Illyria, disguises herself as a page-boy, Cesario, and presents herself at
the doorstep of the house of the local Duke, Orsino. Orsino takes her in and, surmising that she
(or rather he, the made-up person of Cesario) is
bright and eloquent, enlists her/him to help woo
the neighbouring Countess Olivia, with whom he,
Orsino, is in love. Viola, herself instantly smitten
by Orsino, goes and presents herself (again, as
Cesario) now at the doorstep of Olivia, to plead
Orsino's suit. Olivia's not interested in Orsino but
falls quickly in love with (as she thinks) Cesario.
Halfway through their dialogue, the following
exchange takes place:

VIOLA

If I did love you in my master's flame,
With such a suff'ring, such a deadly life,
In your denial I would find no sense;
I would not understand it.

OLIVIA

Why, what would you?

VIOLA

Make me a willow cabin at your gate,
And call upon my soul within the house;
Write loyal cantons of contemned love,
And sing them loud even in the dead of night;
Halloo your name to the reverberate hills,
And make the babbling gossip of the air
Cry out 'Olivia!' O, you should not rest
Between the elements of air and earth
But you should pity me.

How many thresholds are at play here? I lose count. Portals to houses approached and crossed; borders of identity traversed; of gender (doubly so: Viola, reinvented as Cesario, switches from woman to boy – but in the Elizabethan theatre she'd have been played by a boy in the first place); and then, even as not-herself, as this self-decreated character Cesario, s/he imagines him-herself as a double of Orsino, *again on the threshold*, building a willow cabin at Olivia's gate, the boundary to her estate – and, what's more, from there calling to his-her soul within the property. We're back in Lynchean territory here: Call me. Viola-Cesario's lover-persona, from outside the house, will dial in to his soul inside: he's in both places at once, decentred, ec-static. Viola next envisages a schiz-oid filling up of all space with Olivia, or rather with Viola-as-Cesario-as-putative-Orsino/not-Ors-ino-lover-crying-Olivia's-name, until the hills and air themselves become personified and amorous: psychosis and ecstasy merged and apotheosed in a great fugue. There follows a short, economic round to the exchange. After Viola's done perorating, the script continues:

OLIVIA

You might do much.
What is your parentage?

VIOLA

Above my fortunes, yet my state is well

Olivia's question expresses the ubiquitous Shakespearean concern with status and wealth. Viola's response (I'm from a richer background than my current circumstances would suggest, but despite my economically diminished state, I'm happy) asserts the very thing that Carson identifies as ecstasy's condition: poverty.

N ow, perhaps, is the time to return, after a long absence – to trample, or, more grace-fully, to surf our way back in – to Bachmann's poem. Its overall mood – dark, rainy, salty – is one of not joy but melancholy. But, following the line of thinking we've just been pursuing, we should by now have learnt to see the distinction between these two moods as ultimately superficial. Just as jealousy, for Carson's Sappho, is a stepping stone, a portal opening to something else, so here, too, is melancholia. What is that something else? Again, ec-stasis. Let's look at the lines again:

Into the hand of my oldest friend
I place the key to my post; the rain man will now manage
my darkened house and lengthen
the lines of the ledger which I drew up
since I stayed less often.

The stanza speaks of self-expulsion, of auto-dislodging: I'm leaving my home, handing over the management of my household, my *oikos*, business affairs, to the rain man. Who's the rain man? Hard to say: some kind of vague Germanic mythological figure – the very type you could imagine popping up dwarfish and pale-faced and outing with something like 'It is not my custom to go where I am not wanted'. This sequence of events (departure from somewhere; an opening up of the clearly-defined individual to the more vaguely, darkly symbolic) is one that recurs in many of Bachmann's poems. Indeed, *Borrowed Time* begins with one called 'Journey Out' ('Ausfahrt'), whose speaker, leaving a territory, looks back from her ship at a smouldering landscape. 'Vom Lande steigt Rauch auf', its first line reads: Smoke rises from the land, the earth – and, in the post-War context in which Bachmann's writing, from the Land, the country, Germany-Austria, the *Anschluss*-creation that produced so much smoke before going up in smoke itself. 'Journey Out' also contains, a few stanzas later, the image of a tree 'which defiantly lifts an arm' in an all-too-familiar salute. Charles Simic, in his foreword to the Zephyr Press edition, notes that 'Bachmann had a way of writing about nature such that it reminded one of concentration camps'. 'Salt and Bread' does exactly that. Its first two lines read:

> Now the wind sends its rails ahead;
> we will follow in slow trains

What is being hallooed to the reverberate hills here is (as with the house of Atreus) trauma, transmitted on a wavelength that mangles and blurs the mythological with the historical, the psychic with the topographical: all these, like so many burrows running up against each other, start to overlap. Just as 'Journey Out' is full of Iphigenian imagery, of blood trails in a sea whose white-foamed lashes stare back at the gazer ('you should have dug into the sandbank / or tied yourself to the cliff with a strand of hair', she writes), 'Salt and Bread', too, is stuffed with sacrificial ciphers: 'fever-white vestments', a thorn torn 'from the flesh of cactus' and (as per Iphigenia again) seascapes: cliffs and islands, 'tides of truth' that 'will arrive no less often'. Then, as we've seen, from out of this littoral-maritime tableau emerge these lines:

So I gather the salt
when the sea overcomes us,
and turn back
and lay it on the threshold
and step into the house.

I see this volte-face as a counterpart or ana-
logue to the arriving (that is, re-arriving) tides of
truth. The absconded poet-narrator gathers salt
like evidence, each grain a residue of pain, of tears,
of that which 'overcomes us', expanded to a global
scale: the tear-deposits of not individual emotions
but the oceans of the world. She then carries it
back to the 'house' from which it all began, and
lays it on this house's threshold – like Cassandra,
enunciating through poetic gesture, bearing witness cryptically ('Evidence / evidence', Cassandra
chants in Carson's version to the chorus who try
not to understand her); or, perhaps, as though the
bundle held not salt but unacknowledged off-
spring, issuing through the laying-down of it a call
to take responsibility: *This is yours; recognise it!* She
then re-enters the property – no longer 'my house'
but 'the house', one whose 'post', that is, whose
communications, are being managed by the rain
man, this other creation or self-decreation.

Placing 'the key to my post' into the rain man's hand is how Filkins renders Bachmann's line; another translator, Robert Woodhouse, has the speaker 'resign my office' to her old friend. Here it's worth pulling up the original:

In die Hand meines ältesten Freunds leg ich
mein Amt zurück; es verwaltet der Regenmann
jetzt mein finsteres Haus und ergänzt
im Schuldbuch die Linien, die ich zog,
seit ich seltener blieb.

Amt, the main term in question here, has a bureaucratic or official, legislative sense: *authority, department, bureau*, as in *Finanzamt* (tax authority) or *Standesamt* (registry office). *Verwaltet* in the same line for 'manage' (or for Woodhouse, 'take over') has a similar connotation: a *Hausverwaltung* is the company that manages your building; *öffentliche Verwaltung* is public administration and so on. But to relinquish or pass on *authority* has a heightened or doubled, self-reflective nuance when the speaker is, as here (to some extent at least), the proxy for an author. In this respect, there's another crucial slippery key-word hiding from us in the German. In Bachmann's telling, the communication or admin and record-keeping functions of the house are manifested by two things: on the one hand, as we've seen, the post or office (*Amt*); and, on the other, the *ledger* which the speaker used to keep or draw up (and even then, not when in full-time occupancy but rather 'since I stayed less often') but the task of maintaining which she has now ceded to the rain man. For this object – the ledger, the account-pad – Bachmann uses, rather than the standard *Hauptbuch*, the less common alternative *Schuldbuch*. The literal translation for this, chiming with the object's economic function, would be 'debt-book'; but an equally literal (or literal-minded) rendering would be 'guilt-book'. Just as the English *guilt* retains historical associations with gilt currency, in German the concepts of *guilt* and *debt* are rendered by one and the same term: *Schuld*.

Schuldbuch. In the architecture of Bachmann's poem, this word bears an enormous weight. Given that the work is clearly (as I mentioned) self-reflective, a skewed parable that allegorises the work of the poet, and of poetry itself – a manifesto, almost – whose main tasks include the gathering and presentation of grief's traces and the writing down (or lengthening) of lines on a succession of pages, then the logic, rationale or credo it expresses could be paraphrased as follows: the ledger, the decreative writing surface on which I can only write once I'm not there in the position to write it any more, but rather have dislodged myself and handed over that office to someone or something else – this ledger is an index of a guilt which (though not mine alone, but open, general) indebts me, impoverishes me, turns me inside out, to the extent that what I share with outside, roofless and rained on even in my house, my *oikos*, is more debt. The final couplet once more:

> We share bread with the rain;
> bread, a debt, and a house.

Or at least, that's how it stands in the *first* Zephyr edition, from 2006. In the second, which appeared in 2024, Filkins has swapped two words out for another:

> We share bread with the rain;
> bread, guilt, and a house.

The original, of course, requires no such decision, since both meanings are already present:

37

Wir teilen ein Brot mit dem Regen,
ein Brot, eine Schuld und ein Haus.

For Bachmann, this arrangement names the
dare, the venture, the condition of poetic thought
and enunciation.

– 6 –

'Salt and Bread', a stunning work in its own right, also serves (I'd suggest) as a blueprint for Bachmann's magnum opus, her most read and translated work, the one for which she remains internationally famous: *Malina*. Bachmann conceived this novel as the first part of a trilogy that was to bear the title *Todesarten* or 'Death Styles', but died not long after the first installation's publication, following a fire in her Rome villa. I want to spend the final section of this book unpacking what we've already unpacked from 'Salt and Bread', Aeschylus, Carson, Lynch and all the rest over into *Malina* – into or, perhaps, through it, and beyond.

Like 'Salt and Bread' – and, indeed, the majority of Bachmann's poems – *Malina* is written in the first person. And, without falling into the trap of presuming an equivalence between its speaking voice and author, it's fair to say that it both contains and broadcasts a large autobiographical dimension. Its protagonist, whose name we never learn (although her first initial is I), is a successful Austrian writer born in Klagenfurt and living in Vienna, juggling demands for interviews, invitations for foreign lecture-tours and the like, which she more often than not fends off or delays or cancels (as did Bachmann: it's striking how much of her published correspondence with Paul Celan is dedicated to the postponement of rendezvous, the withdrawal from conferences and so forth). This narrator plans, as Bachmann did, to write a great cycle of novels, possibly with the selfsame title, *Todesarten*. She lives in Ungargasse (Hungary Street), in Vienna's Third District, having moved there from the parallel street Beatrixgasse, on which Bachmann in fact lived from 1946 to 1949. There's no 'conventional' or nineteenth-century plot arc in *Malina*: rather, reflections, memories, accounts of curtailed or aborted trips are stitched together in a hybrid patchwork in which narrative prose, dramatic dialogue, epistolary monologue, journalistic transcript, fairytale pastiche and even musical notation thread into and out of one another. The novel's main 'drama', though, resides in the struggle, in the protagonist's life and psyche, between two male figures to whom she's alternately drawn: the upbeat, optimistic Ivan (with whom she's conducting an intense affair) and her elusive and sinister flatmate Malina (who may or may not actually exist). As she moves from the orbit of the second to that of the first then back again, dark and abyssal depths gape open and consume her, culminating in her agonised mental and physical unravelling.

Like so many of the works we've looked at here, *Malina* revolves around a house, around the passage between its inside and its outside, the confusion of these spaces. For the protagonist, the small patch of real estate in and around her Ungargasse home is not merely a place of residence but 'my own land, my country above all others . . . my Ungargassenland, which I must hold, fortify, my only country which I must keep secure . . .' She continues, in language that could come straight from *The Burrow*:

This little piece of side street is my greatest security; during the day I run up the stairs, at night I fall upon the outside door armed with the key, and once again that blissful moment returns, when the key twists, the latches unlock, the door opens and that feeling of having come home overwhelms me in the spray of traffic and people. This sensation radiates across one or two hundred yards where everything signals my house.

Like Kafka's creature's bunker, which has other, 'small fry' creatures whistling in its walls, it's (being an apartment building) shared – an arrangement with which the protagonist, no less than Kafka's subterranean narrator, is uncomfortable: 'living with other people in one house', she tells us, 'is enough to scare you'. Ringing phones attached to lines on which as many as four people might be talking all at once, an opera singer down the hallway, not to mention fridge and bathtub noises and those of the radio and record-player, make the Ungargasse house a polyphonic or cacophonous zone – one that is doubled, or expanded, in what the narrator repeatedly calls 'the House of Austria'. Sitting at a geographical, historical and political crossroads at which Teutonic, Slavic and Muslim cultures all run up against each other, Vienna is a polyglottal place, a switchboard bedevilled by constant linguistic overlap and interference. The narrator and Malina, both hailing from near the Yugoslavian border, converse in a German peppered with Slovenian or Windish; Ivan speaks with his children in Hungarian and (when he doesn't want them to understand him) with the narrator in English; guests at salon dinners shuffle between French and German. Like Joyce's Dublin, or the pages of William Gaddis's *J R* (which it predates by four years), *Malina* is full of babble (often unassigned) – babble that carries variously (or simultaneously) gossip, tender words, news of revolutions and catastrophes, ads, general junk-noise:

So that your world never gets too small for you, there's PRESTIGE, a seabreeze from a far horizon. Everyone is talking about mortgages. You're in good hands with us, proclaims a Mortgage-Bank, you'll go a long way in TARRACO shoes. We coat your Venetian blinds twice so you'll never have to varnish them again, a CALL-Computer is never alone! And then the Antilles, le bon voyage. That's why the Bosch EXQUISITE is one of the best dishwashers in the world. The moment of truth is coming when customers ask our experts questions, when management technique, calculation, net profits, packaging machines, delivery times are all up for debate, VIVIOPTAL for those who can't remember a thing . . .

Note, even in the most trite-sounding of these pitches, the undertones of exile, blindness, cleansing, revelation and forgetting which they carry. The narrator is acutely receptive to such voices; of the requests to help flood victims in northern

Germany and Romania, revolutionaries in Mexico and La Paz and Berlin, and other miscellaneous solicitations to which she devotes much time and attention, Malina complains that she 'brings them into the house, with the Bulgarians, the Germans, the South Americans . . . all these people, the geological and meteorological fronts' – an interesting metaphor which frames the importuning missives, in their overall amalgam, as something akin to rain, bearing down on the house which, as per 'Salt and Bread', is in no state to keep them out.

The house, then, the house in Austria, the House of Austria, is a porous chamber reverberating with all kinds of signals – but there is a bass tone, a base theme, that runs through all of these. 'I'll tell you a terrible secret,' the narrator confides to a journalist interviewing her for the *Vienna Evening Edition*, 'language is punishment. It must encompass all things and in it all things must again transpire according to guilt and the degree of guilt [*Schuld*, both times].' No less than Atreus's, the House of Austria has witnessed, indeed hosted, 'shameful deeds'; and in consequence, no less than Atreus's, it's a crypt. Bachmann uses that word repeatedly; Vienna's palaces, castles and museums she bundles together under the label 'our necropolis'. Malina (to the extent that he functions as an actual person) works as an archivist in the Austrian Army Museum, the building that contains, among other things, the car in which Franz Ferdinand was assassinated – the event that sparked off World War One (from a historical perspective, the House of Austro-Hungary was indeed the place where things went wrong). In the same interview, the narrator proclaims her dislike for 'every administration [*Verwaltung*] . . . this worldwide bureaucracy which has taken over everything from man and his likeness to the potato bug with its carbon copies', before adding: 'But here in Vienna something else is going on, the cultic administration [the Anglo-French loan-word *Administration* this time] of an Empire of the Dead'; then concluding, in an aphorism that the interviewer will refuse to publish: 'Vienna's crematorium is its spiritual mission'.

All these scenes and exchanges take place in *Malina*'s relatively stable (in the sense of occupying a reality field that's constant) first section, 'Happy with Ivan'. In its second, 'The Third Man', though, their contents and themes erupt across a baroque, hallucinatory landscape whose contours and terms are in continual, disorienting flux. 'This time,' the narrator informs us, 'the place is not Vienna. It

is a place called Everywhere and Nowhere.' The
house, the city morph into abyssal landscapes in
which fields and courtyards give over to gas chambers. There follow scenes of incest and familial
abuse, the very Sylvia Plath-like image (Bachmann
wrote a short essay on Plath in 1968) of the narrator's Nazi father ripping out her tongue after, in
a skewed reprisal of a conversation about wisdom
teeth and dentists that took place with Ivan's children earlier, removing all hers. In similar vein, a
set-piece sequence from the first section featuring
a Wolfgangsee regatta, its preoccupations with
reef-trimming and manipulation of the wind ('He
has his own personal gust!' one aristocratic yacht
captain complains of another), transforms into a
nightmarish series of tableaux featuring cold lakes,
frozen lakes, the narrator abandoned by her father
on an island ('I'm cut off, I'm alone, no, no more
ships!') swallowing water as she begs him over the
telephone to rescue her. This is pure Iphigenia. On
the shores of one lake lies 'the cemetery of the murdered daughters'; on those of another, or perhaps
the same, 'dead daughters stand with blowing hair';
the lake becomes the Danube, the Black Sea, the
father a Nile crocodile, jaws dripping with shreds
of flesh; 'old blood is floating on the water, but fresh

blood as well', we're told. If it's Iphigenia, it's Thyestes too, devouring his own young: a courthouse scene depicts the father cutting a schnitzel underneath a cross, drinking red wine, holding a napkin, then donning a butcher's bloodstained apron, then a hangman's coat, then shiny black boots in front of barbed wire, in a watchtower – again, the historical and mythological, the psychic and political, the sacred and profane all interweaving in a general, dissociative fugue.

Or, in fact, *associative*. Amidst all the second section's phantasmagoria and mental disintegration, there's a sense that things are – in the manner of a detective novel, a Whodunnit almost – being pieced together. 'Something is dawning on me, I'm beginning to see some logic,' the narrator mumbles during a moment of lucidity. As in 'Salt and Bread', some tide of truth is being both purveyed and withdrawn in intermittent pulses, some evidence being held in dilute form that might be extracted and gathered, brought back to the house, brought into focus, a coherent, integrated vision. To this end, Malina plays a central role, acting as confidant and therapist, plying the narrator with both sedatives (Bachmann was herself addicted to these by the end of her life) and probing questions, midwife to the epiphany she seems on the verge of having. He alone can read her illegible handwriting; at one point she signs to him in 'the International Language of the Deaf'. The communication between them takes place on a cryptic frequency – and as such there's also something sinister and moribund, almost nefarious, about it. In the third section, 'Last Things', which returns us to the fixed reality of Vienna and the Ungargasse flat but despite that is still dominated by a sense of danger and impending doom, the narrator writes of Malina:

And nonetheless he sometimes scares me because his view of a person is founded in the greatest, most comprehensive knowledge, impossible to acquire at any given place or time and impossible to impart to others . . . behind everything that's said he also appears to hear things unsaid – also that which is said too often.

He's omniscient, omnipresent, yet at the same time hardly there. Ivan, a frequent visitor to the flat, has never physically seen him; at the basic level of scenography Bachmann plays little tricks like having Malina drink only from the narrator's glass, eat only from her plate and extinguish cigarettes only in her (not Ivan's) ashtray, adding (on the face

of it superfluously and therefore on reflection sin-
isterly): 'I conclude nothing'. Both in her house
and not there, he even insists at one point that she
'make one more phone call'. Mystery Malina,* rain
Malina. A recurrent concern in Bachmann's novel
is the management of household finances, accounts
and correspondence. Files marked VERY URGENT,
URGENT, INVITATIONS, REJECTIONS, RECEIPTS,
PAID BILLS, UNPAID BILLS pile up on the narrator's
bureau; her secretary spends most of her time 'filling out forms for me, handling my accounts which
are in an incredible mess', or typing letters under
dictation. *Amt*, in other words. The third section
opens with a long, meditative riff on post and post-
men, the 'wonder of mail, the delivery of letters and

---

* In fact, once you start looking at *Malina* through Lynch goggles,
or Lynch through Bachmann ones, it becomes harder and harder to
think that Lynch hasn't read and taken inspiration from the novel.
The book's not-quite-therapy sessions between a troubled woman
and a quiet man whose role is ill-defined will seem familiar to anybody who's watched *Inland Empire*; the final section's protracted
leaving-the-flat-not-leaving-the-flat discussion, its fraught reversals
in the hallway, will recall a similar scene between Audrey and her
partner/analyst/hallucinated minder in *Twin Peaks: The Return*.
Most tellingly, the quasi-mystical blue cube that appears in the run-
up to the narrator's 'murder' crops up in identical form and circumstances (murder) in *Mulholland Drive*.

packages. Also the neat rows of mailboxes in the front hall', which develops into a fervent defence of a rogue postman who, according to newspaper reports, has been imprisoned for stuffing his flat from floor to ceiling with the very missives whose delivery the Austrian Postal Service had entrusted to him, and whom Bachmann hails, with one eye firmly fixed on Melville's Bartleby, as a heroic modern figure. Who holds the keys to the post? Who gets to manage (*verwalten*) the affairs of a house? Just as the protagonist's intimacy and allegiance oscillate throughout the novel between (on the one hand) Ivan, a more conventional household figure, father of two children who 'pursues his neatly ordered affairs in a building on the Kärtnerring' that, 'since it deals with money', frames him as a symbol of all *oikos* and *oikonomeia*, and (on the other) the liminal, extra- or infra-domestic Malina, so, too, does the authority over – and, by extension, co-authorship of – the lines of what we might also call a *Schuldbuch*, ledger, an 'account' which is to come, one that the text of *Malina* keeps promising to us (but with which it is not itself identical).

Before circling back to this point, crossing its threshold for a final time, I want to make one last digression. It will be through Joyce's 1922 novel

Ulysses, a work to which Bachmann cryptically but unmistakably alludes by having *Malina*'s narrator sample its closing words ('After one sentence Ivan has raised me again, has uplifted me, soothed my skin, gratefully I assent, I say yes. Yes, I said yes.'). *Ulysses*, as its title suggests, follows an Odyssean circuit of departure and return: Leopold Bloom leaves his house in the morning, wanders around Dublin (which Joyce characterises again and again as a necropolis, an Empire of the Dead) selling ad-space for the very type of products with whose praises *Malina*'s narrator's ears are intermittently assailed, and musing, among other things, about a possible story, a murder-mystery detective thriller, he might one day write for money. Economics infiltrates the book at every turn. The son of a money-lender, Bloom not only habitually dreams up get-rich-quick schemes but, ever-inquisitive, has even marked the edge of a florin 'for circulation on the waters of civic finance, for possible, circuitous or direct return'. At the end of his peripatetic day, in the small hours, his last act before retiring is to jot down, in double-entry form (credit in one column, debit in the other), the day's earnings and expenditure in his account book, his ledger. He performs this feat after breaking into his own house (since he is keyless) in the company of the young writer Stephen Dedalus, who, as Dublin's self-declared bard-in-waiting (and a blatant proxy-figure for Joyce himself), has been tasked repeatedly throughout the day, both by himself and others, with composing the great, epic account of his society and era; but who, drunk, homeless and in debt to just about every other character in the novel, has made no more headway than a 'capful of light odes' published in various small magazines and (in the last twenty-four hours) a couple of lines scrawled on a letter someone else has (after lecturing him on economic self-sufficiency) handed to him for delivery.

Bloom, bumbling across his threshold, writes, lengthens some lines. Within the book's larger symbolic economy, this small act of accounting stands in (much as it does in 'Salt and Bread') for the much bigger one, the great 'account' to come – stands in, that is, for *Ulysses* itself, and, beyond that, for the very possibility of epic modern writing. To stay within these symbolic or allegorical parameters – in other words, to read the homecoming and ledger-writing set-up allegorically, as a cryptic schema or embedded manifesto for the larger project of which it forms part – we could hear in it the following proposition: that it is only as one approaches (re-approaches) one's house with or *as* a stranger with whom bread and debt are shared (Bloom has been taking care of the incapacitated and penurious Stephen's petty cash while they visit a brothel together; he's also stood him some refreshment at a cab stand on the way home), only as one nears this threshold that this book-to-come looms into view as a potentiality, as something that might realise itself, come into being, what Stephen calls 'a movement, an actuality of the possible as possible'. And to this proposition we might add an observation: it is not the novel's central writer-figure (Stephen) who is shown doing the writing here, but rather (after Stephen has departed the house) the spectral presence (Bloom has all day long been likened to a ghost, called a 'dark horse', or just ignored; the night before he has appeared to Stephen in a dream) that has shadowed him throughout.

So, back to *Malina*. The novel's central stake, the task which the narrator has been set, and of which she is constantly reminded by all those around her, is the composition of a big, important book, the likes of which the world has never before seen. She moulds it in her mind over and over, fantasising it into existence:

A shower of words starts in my head, then a flickering, some syllables begin to glow, and brightly coloured commas fly out of all the dependent clauses and the periods which were once black have swollen into balloons which float up to my cranium, for everything will be like EXSULTATE JUBILATE in that glorious book I am thus just beginning to find. Should this book appear, as someday it must, people will writhe with laughter after just one page, they will leap for joy, they will be comforted, they will read on, biting their fists to suppress their cries of joy, it can't be helped, and when they sit down by the window and read still further they'll begin to throw confetti to the pedestrians on the street, so that they, too, will stop, astonished, as if they had walked into a carnival, and people will start throwing apples and nuts, dates and figs just like St. Nicholas' Day, they will lean out of their windows without getting dizzy and shout out: Hear, hear! look and see! I have just read something wonderful, may I read it to you, everybody come nearer, it's too wonderful!

This imaginary book, this book-to-come, oscillates, as I mentioned earlier, between two versions it could take. The first is the joyous version of which we heard tell above, the version that suggests itself whenever she's in Ivan's orbit – indeed, it's he who comes up with the title *EXSULTATE JUBILATE*. Ivan, she writes, 'has come to make consonants constant once again and comprehensible, to unlock vowels to their full resounding, to let words come over my lips once more', so much so that his name reverberates, just like Olivia's in Viola-Cesario's imagining, about the city's very air. She even starts to compose this version: it's a fairy tale that gathers centuries of European history up into a magical love story. The narrator thinks she might complete it on a old desk that she spots in an antiques shop, on 'old, durable parchment'. But she doesn't buy the desk, and 'wouldn't have been able to write on it anyway, since parchment and ink are not to be found'. Besides which, the few pages of it she actually does pen are deliberately kitsch (*'The princess was very young and very beautiful and rode a black horse whose speed exceeded that of all others'* etc); Bachmann can only bring herself to render them in pastiche form. The second version that the book-to-come could take would be the version that suggests itself when she's in Malina's orbit: dark, melancholic or even dystopian, 'a book', as she puts it in the full throes of her hallucinations, 'about Hell'. Possible titles for this version are *Three Murders*, *Darkness in Egypt*, *DEATH STYLES* and

NOTES FROM A MORGUE. The two versions, it goes without saying, are polar opposites of one another – yet reciprocally counterbalancing. 'I need my double existence,' she writes, 'my Ivanlife and my Malinafield, I cannot be where Ivan isn't, just as I cannot return home when Malina isn't there'; by the same logic, the contending book-versions are both mutually exclusive *and* intimately interlinked, each a kind of flipped or inverse copy of the other.

As *Malina* progresses, though, the logic and aesthetic of the second version get the upper hand. A febrile reprisal of the ballroom scene from *War and Peace* gives over to a conversation in which Malina tells her that 'It isn't war and peace . . . It's war', which exchange sets up the second section's climax:

Malina: So you'll never again say: War and Peace.
Me: Never again.
          It's always war.
          Here there is always violence.
          Here there is always struggle.
          It is the eternal war.

But once again, as we saw earlier, the distinction between these two versions is (I'd argue) ultimately superficial. Why? Because both joy (on the one hand) and (on the other) melancholy or even horror are (as before) passageways that, separately and in conjunction, lead to the staging and experience of a *passion* which is the book's real subject. I use this term, *passion*, in both its amorous and religious senses. No less than 'Salt and Bread', *Malina* is full of sacrificial motifs: crosses, thorns, white vestments. The narrator speaks of being nailed to a cross, and prophesies: 'I shall fall three times before I can rise again'; returning from the 'House of Ivan' to her Ungargasse home, she pauses in the doorway 'leaning against the entrance . . . in my Passion, with the stations of my Passion before my eyes, stations I have again willingly traversed, from his house to my house'. That she stages, here, this passion on her own doorway, that its stations are located in the interval between two houses, presses home (or presses, let's say, to home's threshold) the point that it is an ec-static passion. A few pages later, reprising once again the *War and Peace* ballroom setting, she uses this very adjective:

I am the first perfect extravagance, ecstatic and incapable of putting the world to any reasonable use, and I may show up at the masked ball of society, or stay away like someone who has been detained, or has forgotten to make a mask, or can no longer find his costume out of carelessness, and so one day will no longer be invited. When I stand in front of a familiar door in Vienna, perhaps because I am invited, it occurs to me at the last moment it might be the wrong door, or day or hour, and I turn around and drive back to the Ungargasse, too quickly tired, too much in doubt.

Pausing in doorways, being invited but not present, or present but not invited, home but not at home, turning around or back – it's all there, on repeat. This is the poet-narrator's lot, her fate, her state of being-on-the-threshold: her passion, her ecstasis.

That this passion ends up being tortured, agonised, makes it no less passionate for that – and no less true. The passion elaborated over the course of *Malina* is a faithful response, a faithful rendition or 'account', of a set of conditions both visible and invisible, spoken and muted, which the narrator correctly intuits and maps. Of all versions of the book-to-come that proffer themselves to her – between these and beyond them too – it points towards the only one that's *truly* viable in post-war Austria, this House with so many bodies piled up in its storeroom, and with so much debt, or guilt. Laying herself open to the encrypted, sunken histories of both house and sea, she – like Cassandra moving between stations on her dial – voices their broken, fragmented and perhaps psychotic but nonetheless *true* articulation. At one point, near the end, as she nears her own death, the protagonist makes an (again, cryptic but unmistakable) allusion to Theodore Adorno's epochal assertion (made in 1949) that to write poetry after Auschwitz would be barbaric: 'No day will come, poetry will never and they will never . . .' Hers is a double refusal: the refusal to write *and* the refusal not to. 'I can no longer write the beautiful book, without any reason I have stopped thinking about the book long ago, nothing more comes to me, not a single sentence', we are told – yet from the very silence brought on by that act of abnegation roars the text of *Malina*, a work that's certainly not *EXSULTATE JUBILATE* but also not exactly coterminous with *Three Murders/Darkness in Egypt* etc either. Better to call it, echoing Adorno (author of *Negative Dialectics*) once more, a kind of negative miasma in which both versions are held in unrealised, and perhaps unrealisable, form – all presided over by the ultimate negative figure, the figure of

the negative, or subtraction itself, to whom the protagonist's last words are: 'take over all the stories
which make up history. Take them all away from
me'.

Bachmann's narrator ends the book outside
herself, literally: a final surreal move sees her enter
a crack in the flat's wall and – somehow – take up
residence there. 'On every periphery a woman
is murdered', she has surmised from the news
media's endless reports of femicide; now, from
the periphery of her own domicile she'll observe
her own being-disappeared. The novel's final passage shows Malina alone in the room, clearing her
table ('he lets my coffee cup disappear . . . Only
his small green-rimmed cup is still there, nothing more, proof that he is alone'), tearing up and
crumpling her papers and denying to a caller (perhaps Ivan) that anyone of her name (what name?)
ever lived at that number. Like Cesario (who never
existed either) she builds and takes up her post
in an imaginary cabin at the gate – the boundary,
limen, inside-outside membrane – of Being itself,
and calls out, halloos, from there. This is her final,
reduced state, her ultimate poverty – a decreation
that, even as it makes any further writing in one
sense impossible (no book will come), at the same

time and with the selfsame gesture carries us up to the threshold of both *Malina* and the poetic event-field, all the books-to-come, to which Bachmann's masterpiece opens the door. This ultra-paradoxical situation – 'when', as she puts it, 'I can do and can no longer do, simultaneously' – enacts (to borrow Carson's terms again) the absolute daring that is the impossible condition, and the very possibility, of literature.

– Appendix One –

Agamemnon
A play in two acts by Tom McCarthy

ACT ONE

Lights up to reveal the entrance to a house. This consists of a free-standing doorway (frame only) installed in the middle of the stage and facing along the stage right to stage left axis, i.e. at an angle of exactly ninety degrees to the audience. On the floor immediately to the doorway's left (stage right), a doormat bearing the word WELCOME. Several feet to the doorway's right (stage left), a bath-tub. At the base of the doorway itself, a block of wood or metal three feet long and one and a half inches high. This must be firmly attached to the stage floor.

Enter, from stage right, **Agamemnon**, a man in his mid-forties. He walks from stage right towards stage left in a straight line that runs through the doorway. As he passes through the frame, he trips on the block and falls over.

Lights down.

ACT TWO

Lights half up to reveal a set cleared of doorway, doormat and bathtub, i.e. consisting only of the block. Across the stage's back wall the events of Act One, which have been filmed by a camera installed in front of the stage exactly in line with the doorway, are replayed by means of a video projector. The replay must take place in extreme slow motion, at such a speed that the sequence from Agamemnon's entrance to his arrival at a state of rest on the floor lasts forty minutes.

Lights down.

NOTES

1. Agamemnon's fall must follow the same stage right to stage left trajectory as his walk, so that he falls through and from the frame towards the bathtub, coming to rest face down with his feet pointing back towards the doorway and his hands towards the bathtub.

2. If the video replay equipment being used for the production is not sophisticated enough to replay Act One in extreme slow motion within Act Two immediately, Act One should be filmed and the footage slowed down to the desired speed using appropriate editing software prior to the performance. In this case, the actor playing Agamemnon must ensure that his movements are identical both times he performs Act One.

3. For this version of *Agamemnon*, the camera must be placed among the audience seating exactly in line with the doorway, as stated. The director can, however, choose to stage different versions by placing the camera on the theatre's ceiling directly above the doorway pointing down towards the floor, in which case the play's title for that particular production should be amended to *Agamemnon (Gods)*; or by placing it off stage left pointing across towards stage right, in which case the play's title should be amended to *Agamemnon (Clytemnestra)*; or by using three cameras, one placed in each of the positions indicated above, in which case the play's title should be amended to *Agamemnon (Cassandra)*.

– Appendix Two –

Salt and Bread

Now the wind sends its rails ahead;
we will follow in slow trains
and inhabit these islands,
trust beside trust.

Into the hand of my oldest friend
I place the key to my post; the rain man will now manage
my darkened house and lengthen
the lines of the ledger which I drew up
since I stayed less often.

You, in fever-white vestments,
gather the exiled and tear
from the flesh of cactus a thorn
– symbol of impotence
to which we meekly bow.

We know
that we'll remain the continent's captives,
and again we'll succumb to its troubled ills,
and the tides of truth
will arrive no less often.

For sleeping yet in the cliff
is the barely lit skull,
the claw hangs in the claw
in the dark stone, and the stigmata
are healed in the violet of the volcano.

Of the great storms of light,
none has reached the living.

So I gather the salt
when the sea overcomes us,
and turn back
and lay it on the threshold
and step into the house.

We share bread with the rain;
bread, a debt,* and a house.

(translated by Peter Filkins)

* In the second, revised edition, as we have seen, 'a debt' is
changed to 'guilt'.

Salz und Brot

Nun schickt der Wind die Schienen voraus,
wir werden folgen in langsamen Zügen
und diese Inseln bewohnen,
Vertrauen gegen Vertrauen.

In die Hand meines ältesten Freunds leg ich
mein Amt zurück; es verwaltet der Regenmann
jetzt mein finsteres Haus und ergänzt
im Schuldbuch die Linien, die ich zog,
seit ich seltener blieb.

Du, im fieberweißen Ornat,
holst die Verbannten ein und reißt
aus dem Fleisch der Kakteen einen Stachel
– das Zeichen der Ohnmacht,
dem wir uns willenlos beugen.

Wir wissen,
daß wir des Kontinentes Gefangene bleiben
und seinen Kränkungen wieder verfallen,
und die Gezeiten der Wahrheit
werden nicht seltener sein.

Schläft doch im Felsen
der wenig erleuchtete Schädel,
die Kralle hängt in der Kralle
im dunkeln Gestein, und verheilt
sind die Stigmen am Violett des Vulkans.

Von den großen Gewittern des Lichts
hat keines die Leben erreicht.

So nehm ich vom Salz,
wenn uns das Meer übersteigt,
un kehre zurück
und legs auf die Schwelle
und trete ins Haus.

Wir teilen ein Brot mit dem Regen,
ein Brot, eine Schuld und ein Haus.

– Bibliography –

Aeschylus, *The Oresteia*, trans. Philip Vellacott, London: Penguin, 1956

Gaston Bachelard, *The Poetics of Space*, trans. Maria Jolas, Boston: Beacon Press, 1994

Ingeborg Bachmann, *Darkness Spoken: The Collected Poems of Ingeborg Bachmann*, trans. Peter Filkins, Brookline: Zephyr Press, 2006; *Malina*, trans Philip Boehm, New York: Holmes and Meier, 1999

Mikhail Bakhtin, *Problems of Dostoevsky's Poetics*, trans. Caryl Emerson, Minneapolis: University of Minnesota Press, 1984

Walter Benjamin, *The Arcades Project*, trans. Howard Eiland and Kevin McLaughlin, Cambridge: Harvard University Press, 2002

Anne Carson, *An Oresteia*, London: Faber and Faber, 2010; *Decreation*, New York: Knopf, 2005

Simon Critchley, *Mysticism*, New York: New York Review Books, 2024

Sigmund Freud, *The Uncanny*, trans. David McLintock, London: Penguin Classics, 2003

James Joyce, *Ulysses*, London: Penguin Classics, 2000

Franz Kafka, *The Burrow*, in *Collected Stories*, trans. Willa and Edwin Muir, New York: Schocken, 1946

David Lynch and Chris Rodley, *Lynch on Lynch*, London: Faber and Faber, 1997

Sappho, *If Not, Winter: Fragments of Sappho*, trans. Anne Carson, New York: Knopf, 2002

William Shakespeare, *Twelfth Night, or What You Will*, London: The Arden Shakespeare, 2003

– Acknowledgements –

The origins of this book lie in an invitation, extended to me in 2023 by my fellow novelist Riikka Pelo, to talk at University of the Arts Helsinki. There, I sketched in telegraphic form the implications of twelve lines from Ingeborg Bachmann's poem 'Salt and Bread', tracking their scenes and motifs outwards to various points in Shakespeare, Kafka, Anne Carson, David Lynch and others, in an attempt to draw into view a thematic constellation around the dual figures of threshold and ledger, and the larger framing structure of the house. Towards the seminar's end, Pelo responded with a photo-essay depicting her own retracing of the various villas and apartments in which Bachmann had stayed during her final, ill-fated Rome residency – a compact *ciné-roman* that I hope also to see in print one day, since it provides a visual counterpoint to the thoughts in this book.

Some months later, I was sitting back home in Berlin telling myself I should flesh my notes out properly and wondering where to publish them, when, with perfect dramatic timing (as in those films where, after an expectant beat, the phone rings), I received an email from Notting Hill Editions asking if I might want to do a book-length essay with them. *The Threshold and the Ledger* is the consequence of that second invitation. I'm grateful to Rosalind Porter for helping it find its present form; also to Peter Filkins and Zephyr Press for allowing me to reproduce the former's masterful English translation of Bachmann's poem, and to Piper Verlag for allowing me to reprint the original. Anthony Eagan, my Santa Fe Institute colleague, brought Bakhtin's reflections on Dostoevsky to my attention; to him, and to SFI in general, I'm grateful – as I am to my agents Jonathan Pegg, Melanie Jackson and Marc Koralnik. And, as always, to Eva, Isadora and Alexis Lemon.

Tom McCarthy, Berlin, 2025